Fun for Ten Fingers

Easy pieces and puzzles for young pianists

by

Pauline Hall and Paul Drayton

Illustrations by Caroline Crossland

© Oxford University Press 1995
Impression 24

Music Department
OXFORD UNIVERSITY PRESS
Great Clarendon Street, Oxford OX2 6DP

Printed in China

The Farmer

Cheerfully

Here's the farm - er mak - ing hay, she hopes the sun will shine all day. If it rains and

makes a flood, her trac - tor wheels stick in the mud.

Duet part

Engine driver

Speedily

Why not be an en - gine dri - ver if you have the chance? Whiz - zing through the Chan - nel Tun - nel: next stop, France!

Duet part

Astronaut

Mer - cu - ry, Ve - nus too, Ju - pi - ter, and Mars: Fur - ther still, in - to space, E - ven to the stars.

Duet part

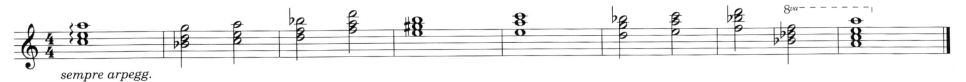

sempre arpegg.

Space (and lines too!)

Some of these notes are in spaces, and some of them are on lines.

Draw a spaceship beside each space note.

Join the line notes with a railway line:

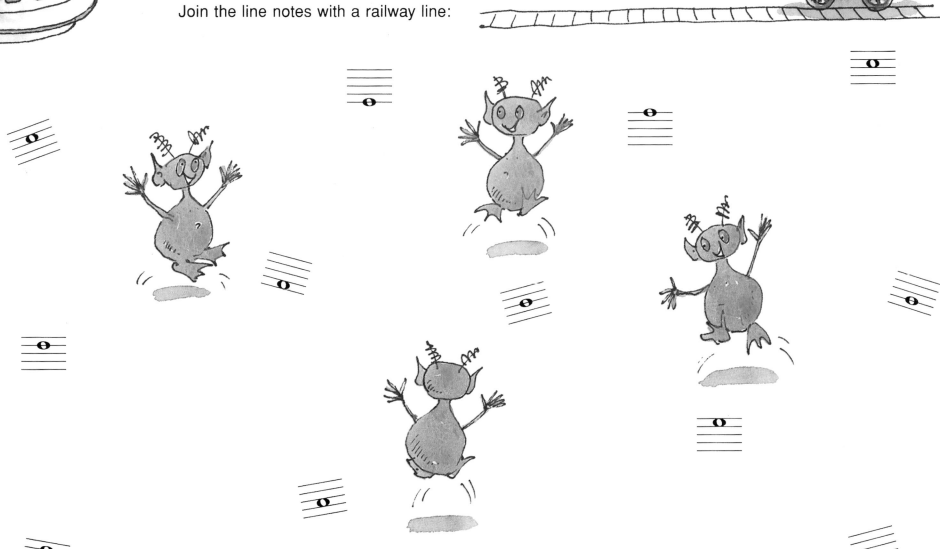

Ghost

Before you play, can you spot two B flats?

Spookily

I'm the ghost of the haunt-ed house— I'll try to give you a fright. As long as I ne-ver

meet a mouse, I'll keep it up all night. woooooo!

Duet part

ffz

Make up your own ghost tune

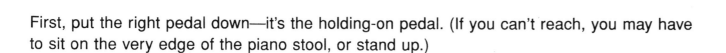

First, put the right pedal down—it's the holding-on pedal. (If you can't reach, you may have to sit on the very edge of the piano stool, or stand up.)

Then put your left hand over these five keys—choose a set low down at the end of the piano, so that they will sound very deep and mysterious.

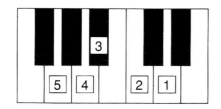

Play them in a clump all together—sshh!—as quietly as you can.

Put your right hand over these keys:

Play the notes in any order—very slowly and very quietly. It must sound like a ghost creeping through the shadows.

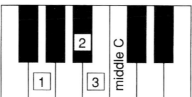

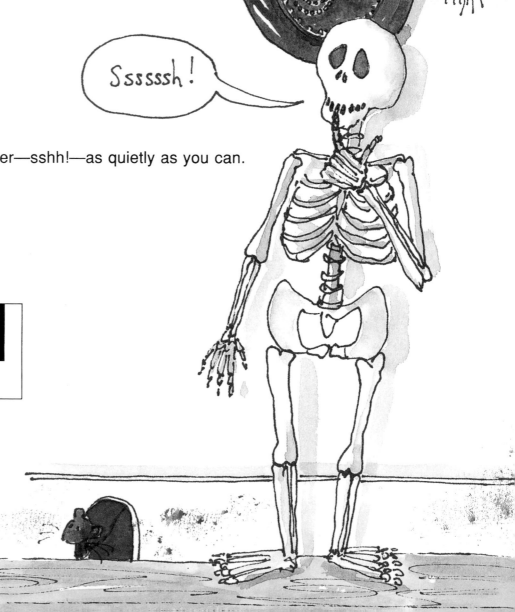

Try adding some extra notes. Keep the pedal pressed down all the time!

Postman

Ploddingly

Here comes the post-man Joe, trud-ging through the rain and snow; carry-ing in his great big sack a post-card sent by

Un - cle Jack.

Duet part

News from China

Write your name and address here.

POSTCARD

Hope you're well. China is a beautiful place. I have been listening to some Chinese music. Perhaps you'll be able to play it. Love from Uncle Jack.

Traditional Chinese music is often based on a pentatonic (five-note) scale. Use the black keys on the keyboard to create your own pentatonic tune. Here's how to do it:

Use five black keys—three for your left hand, two for your right.

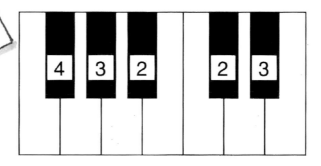

Get your fingers ready over the black keys. You can play them in any order but end with the bottom note (4th fingers, left hand).

Now play a tune to fit these words:

Chinese lanterns sparkling bright
In the darkness of the night.

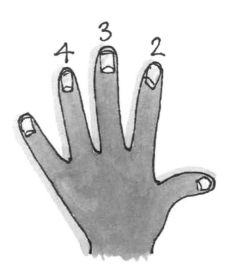
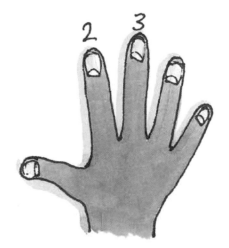

Try playing it with the notes in a different order.

Monster

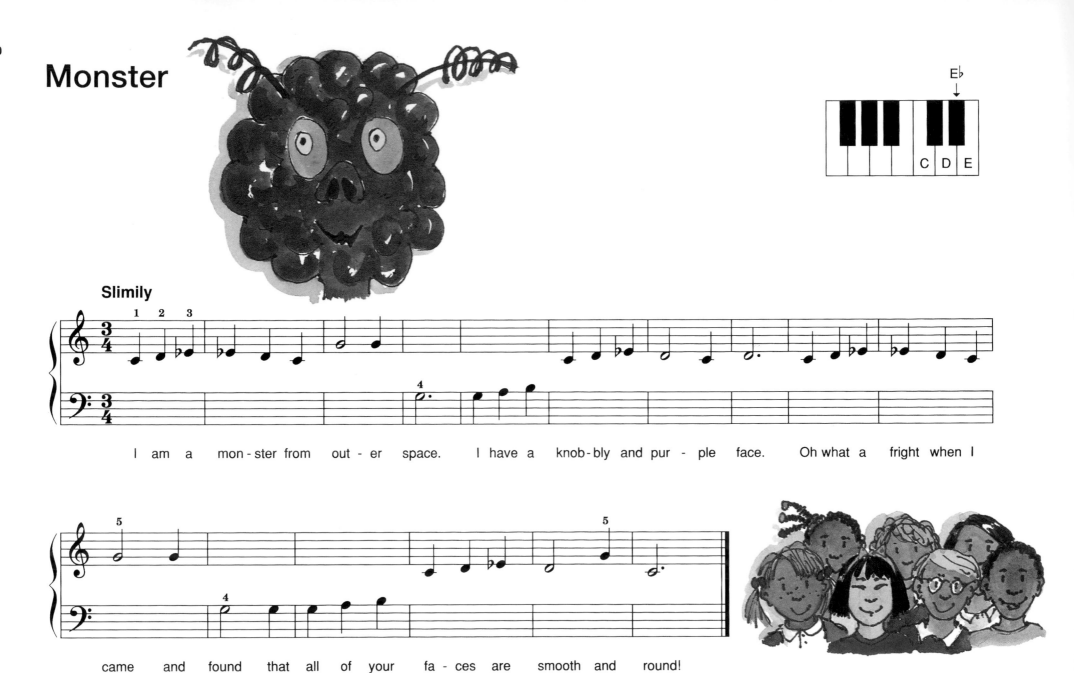

Slimily

I am a mon-ster from out-er space. I have a knob-bly and pur - ple face. Oh what a fright when I

came and found that all of your fa - ces are smooth and round!

Duet part

Are you a good listener? Can you remember things?

Try this listening game:

Play this note:

Take it off and *think* the sound of it.
Wait . . . then sing it!

Play it again—was your
singing note the same?

Try another 'listen and remember':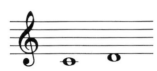

Wait while you remember . . .
sing the notes . . .

Play them again. Well done!

Try some more 'play and sing' games—you'll get better at doing them!

Santa Claus

Your right hand plays
F sharp five times.

Spikily

San - ta Claus comes down the chim - ney look - ing fat and jol - ly. He sinks in - to a com - fy chair up - on a sprig of hol - ly!

Duet part

A Christmas carol to play

Merrily

We wish you a mer-ry Christ-mas, we wish you a mer-ry Christ-mas, we wish you a mer-ry Christ-mas and a

hap-py New Year. Good ti-dings we bring to you and your kin; we wish you a mer-ry Christ-mas and a

hap-py New Year!

Pirate

Breezily

I am a pi-rate bold: In my ship are piles of gold. I sing a pi-rate song, drink-ing rum the whole day long.

Duet part

The pirates have found a cave with lots of things washed up from a sunken ship. But not all of them are treasure—in fact some of them are quite wrong!

Draw a treasure chest  beside the things that are right.

Draw a skull and crossbones  beside the things that are wrong. Good luck!

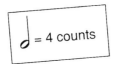 = 4 counts

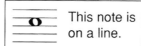 This note is on a line.

 a sharp sign

 getting softer

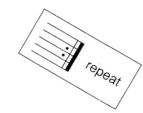 repeat

 Top line F

 Middle D

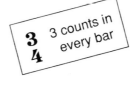 3 counts in every bar

 short and jumpy

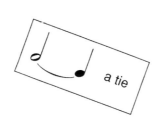 a tie

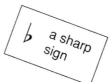 G

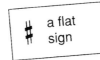 a treble clef

 a flat sign

 getting louder

 a 1 count rest

3 counts

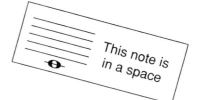 This note is in a space

TV Journalist

Watch as the T V jour - nal - ist brings all the ex - ci - ting news, A weath - er re - port and

all the sport With some live - ly in - ter - views.

Duet part

When Jane the TV Journalist reads the news she will often talk to journalists in other countries.
Here are five of those countries, hidden as musical notes. Can you work out what they are?

Clowns

Playfully

Here comes the clown with her fun - ny red nose and her shoes that could real - ly be short - er. Here comes an - oth - er one

bring - ing a hose, and he drench - es the first one with wa - ter.

Duet part

Sweet shop

This is a game to play with someone else—perhaps your teacher.

In this sweet shop there are lots of jars of sweets, but the labels have all come off and just the rhythm of the name is left.

Can you choose the right label for each jar? Take it in turns to clap a rhythm and match it to its label. Then write the number of the label on its jar. Have a yummy time!

One or two jars have the same rhythm.

1 TOFFEES

3 MARSH MALLOWS

2 Jelly babies

4 Liquorice Allsorts

5 Pink Sugar Mice

7 Fudge

6 WINE GUMS

8 Lollipops

9 Peanut Brittle

10 Peppermint creams

Scarecrow

Lonely

Here in the field I stand all day, try-ing to keep the birds a-way. Still they are com-ing from east and

west, tak-ing my straw to build a nest.

Duet part

Steps and skips

When you play next-door notes like this: 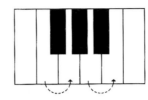 it's a STEP.

When you play two notes with one in between like this: 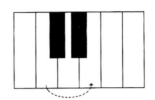 it's a SKIP.

Now for an adventure! Where will you end up?

Follow the instructions given for each hand below. You can use one finger (or more if you like).
Try not to look at the keyboard—feel your way if you're not sure where to go.

Right Hand

Start on middle C. Then go

up a STEP . . . then

up a SKIP . . . go on . . .   — Where did
you land?

up a SKIP . . . on you go . . .

down a STEP.

Left Hand

Start on middle C. Go on

down a STEP . . .

down a SKIP . . .   — Where did
you land?

up a STEP . . .

up a SKIP.

Try some more of your own, starting on different notes. Where do you get to?

Pilot

Right hand plays black E flat,
left hand plays black B flat.

Swoopily

I am an ae - ro - plane pi - lot who knows e - ver - y ae - ro - plane trick. Some - times I

fly in a loop and then all the peo - ple are sick. — Ugh!

Duet part

Jumping around

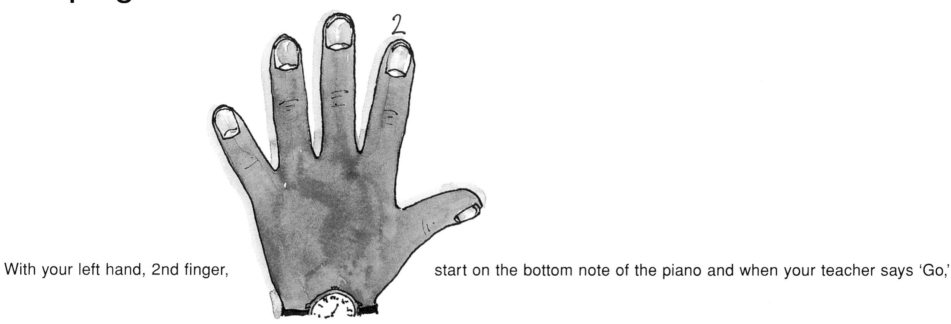

With your left hand, 2nd finger, start on the bottom note of the piano and when your teacher says 'Go,' jump onto each of the *white* keys in turn, as far as middle C. Then let your right hand take over from middle C to the top of the piano. Go as fast as you can, but if you miss a note or trip up, you must go back to the beginning and start again.

Next—with your right-hand 2nd finger, start at the top of the piano and jump down onto every *black* key until you reach the lowest one. Then it's your left hand's turn to jump up each of the *black* keys, starting at the lowest one, until you reach the top.

Now both hands have a go.

Start with both 2nd fingers side-by-side on middle C. When your teacher says 'Go!' hop them away from each other.
How long are your arms? How far can you reach?

Lastly, find all the F sharps on the piano and play them. Then find and play all the B flats.

You've had quite a lot of exercise!

Footballer

Keenly

Speed-y Stan the foot-ball man he shows no fear. He aims and shoots with his great big boots and the crowd all cheer!____

Duet part

The Great Scorer

Can you kick a goal? Then try this game.

Beside every goal is the letter-name of a note. If you can draw it on its own line or in its own space, you score!
If you get it wrong, it's a penalty.

The first one is done for you to show you how.

Gymnast

B flat and A sharp share
the same black key.

Bendily

Turn-ing cart-wheels on the beam, her bo-dy's like e - las - tic. She's the best in all the team at an-y-thing gym - nas - tic.

Duet part

What did the gymnast win?

She was such a success in the competition that she was awarded something special. Can you discover what it was?

Draw it here:

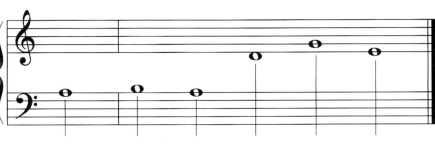

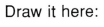

Write the letter-names
of the notes here:

After the competition she had a treat:

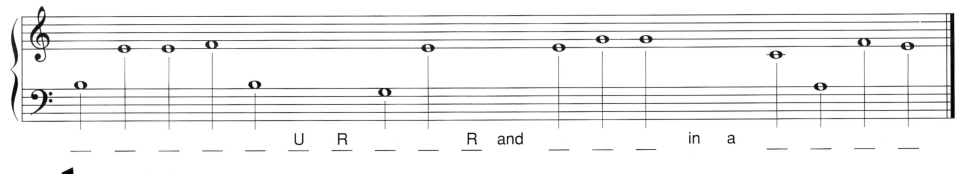

U R   R and _ _ _ _   in a _ _ _ _

Write the letter-names here:

Cowboy

Lazily

The cow - boy drives his cows a - long, he sings a hap - py cow - boy song. Then on his tired old horse he leans, and

tucks in - to a can of beans.

Duet part

A Cowboy Song

Here's a song the cowboy might sing when he's finished tucking into his can of beans.

Home on the Range

Contentedly

Oh give me a home where the buf - fa - lo roam, where the deer and the an - te - lope play._____ Where

ne - ver is heard a dis - cou - ra - ging word, and the skies are not clou - dy all day._____

Magician

Look out for D flat in your right hand!

Mysteriously

Have you seen the great ma - gi - cian make a pound coin dis - ap - pear? Then he says the ma - gic word and

takes it out of some - one's ear!

Duet part

Mysteriously

A magic trick for the piano

Can you make a note sound without actually playing it?

With your right hand, very slowly press down five keys so that they don't make a sound. Keep them held down.
With your left hand, play a low-down key as loudly as you can (*ff*) and staccato.

Listen . . . What can you hear?

Try it again with some different notes. Did it work?

When the magician did his trick, what **MAGIC WORD** did he say?

Write the letter names of the notes here ➔

Snake charmer

Left hand plays 1 black key—A flat
Right hand plays 2 black keys—E flat and F sharp

Charmingly

With my snake and   bas - ket you may   find me quite a - larm - ing.   But   when I play my   ma - gic pipe you'll   find the mu - sic

charm - ing.

Duet part

Try playing this snakey tune.

Make up another
snake-charming tune
of your own!

Gardener

Lots of black flat keys—2 for each hand.

Sunnily

The gar-den-er fet-ches her hose - pipe to wa-ter all the flowers. As soon as she's fi-nished the last

one, the rain comes down for hours!

Duet part

What's happening in the garden?

All these flowers have somehow escaped from their flower pots. Can you put them in their right pots?
Clap or tap their names first. Then write their numbers on the right pot.

1. Marigold

2. Bluebell

3. Rose

4. Daffodil

5. Honeysuckle

6. Snapdragon

7. Lily-of-the-valley

8. Buttercup

9. Snowdrop

10. Water lily

Snooker player

Jazzily

See the fa-mous snoo-ker play-er li-ning up his shi-ny cue. Pot-ting balls of ev-ery col-our: red and black and pink and blue!

Duet part

A snooker puzzle

In snooker:

a RED ball counts as ONE

a YELLOW ball counts as TWO

a GREEN ball counts as THREE

a BROWN ball counts as FOUR

Draw a ring round a musical note that counts

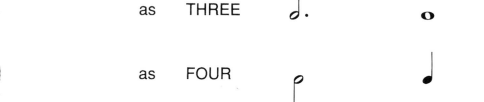

as ONE

as TWO

as THREE

as FOUR

What's your score?

There are four snooker balls in each box. Can you write their notes in the next box and then add up the score?
The first one has been done for you.

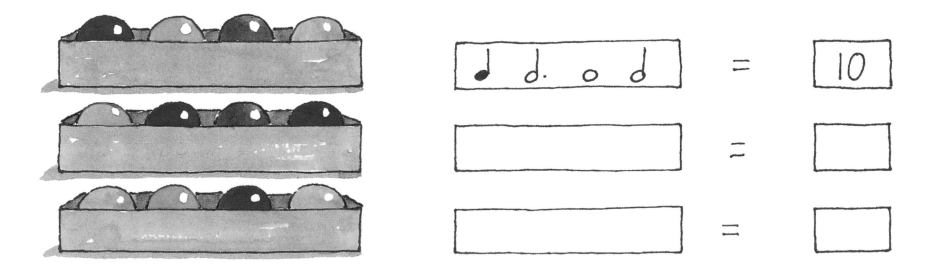

Snowman

Coolly

The snow - man stands in the gar - den with snow right up to his knees: why won't he come in and

warm him - self? He says he'd ra - ther freeze!

Duet part

Staccato, like snowflakes

To end with, here's a well-known march to play:

When the Saints come marching in

Oh when the Saints___ come march-ing in,___ Oh when the Saints come march-ing in,___

___ Oh yes, I want to be in that num-ber,___ when the Saints come march-ing in.___

Duet part

When you have played all the pieces in this book, choose the three that you like best.

Write their names here:

1	
2	
3	

Then play them a lot until you really know them. Why don't you play them to someone and give them a treat?